Peters'-3

Blank Music Book

Easy-to-Remove Sheets

Keyboard Notation   Musical Terms and Signs   Voice Range

10 Staves   56 Pages   Wide Spacing   Dark Lines

Name_____

WILLIS MUSIC

EXCLUSIVELY DISTRIBUTED BY

HAL•LEONARD®
CORPORATION
7777 W. BLUEMOUND RD. P.O. BOX 13819
MILWAUKEE, WISCONSIN 53213

ESSENTIAL MUSICAL FACTS

Music is rhythm, melody and harmony, expressed in sound or TONES.

NOTATION

The first 7 letters of the alphabet are used to name all the NOTES in music — A, B, C, D, E, F, and G. · These NOTES on a written or printed page represent the musical TONES.

Here is a section of the piano keyboard showing how these letters (notes) are repeated, representing the 88 keys on the piano.

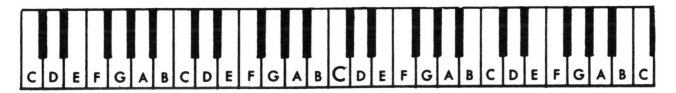

NOTES are written on a STAFF. A staff is made up of five lines and four spaces. The clef sign on the staff tells us the names of the notes on the lines and spaces. There are two commonly used Clefs — G (Treble) and F (Bass).

G Clef

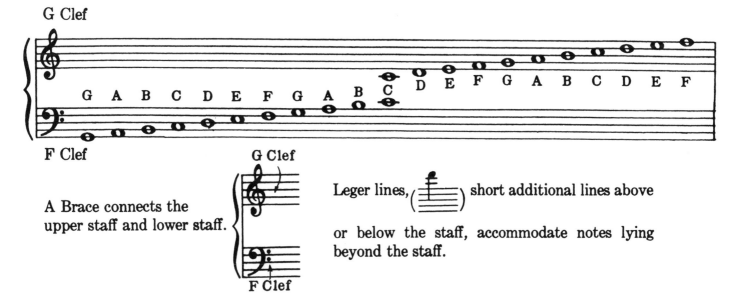

F Clef

A Brace connects the upper staff and lower staff.

G Clef

F Clef

Leger lines, short additional lines above or below the staff, accommodate notes lying beyond the staff.

Music is divided by vertical lines called BARS, (or bar lines) into portions called MEASURES

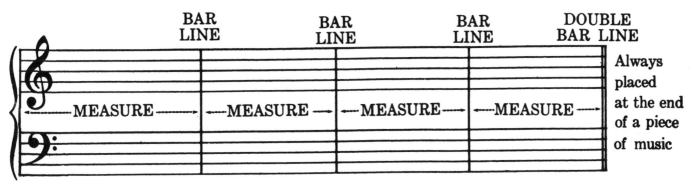

TYPES OF NOTES AND RESTS

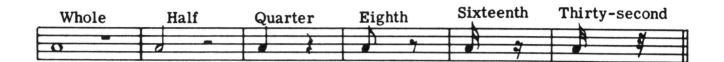

NOTE VALUES:

Whole Note	= 2 Half Notes
Half Note	= 2 Quarter Notes
Quarter Note	= 2 8th Notes
8th Note	= 2 16th Notes
16th Note	= 2 32nd Notes
32nd Note	= 2 64th Notes

When two or more Eighth Notes are joined together, a beam is used instead of the flag.

A DOT placed after a note or rest increases its value by one-half.

TIME SIGNATURE: The two figures at the beginning of a composition are called the TIME SIGNATURE. The top figure tells the number of beats in a measure, and the lower figure tells what kind of note receives one beat. The sign C called Common Time, means four quarter notes in a measure. The sign ¢, called alla breve (al-la-bra-va) means two half notes in a measure.

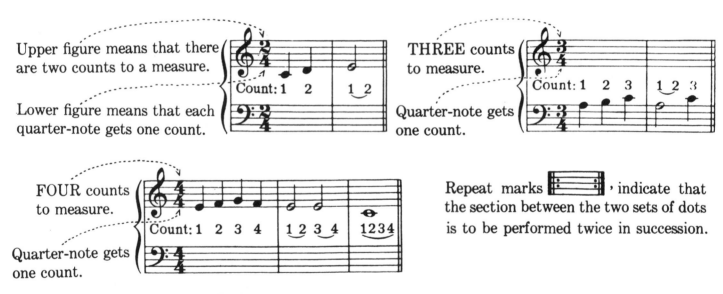

Upper figure means that there are two counts to a measure.

Lower figure means that each quarter-note gets one count.

THREE counts to measure.

Quarter-note gets one count.

FOUR counts to measure.

Quarter-note gets one count.

Repeat marks indicate that the section between the two sets of dots is to be performed twice in succession.

SHARPS, FLATS and NATURALS (Accidentals):

This is called a SHARP: ♯   This is called a FLAT: ♭   This is called a NATURAL (CANCEL): ♮

Each black key can be a sharp or flat. A *sharp* is the black note to the right of the white note and takes its name from the white note, such as F♯ — C♯ — etc. A *sharp* makes a note a *half step higher*.

A *flat* is the black note to the left of the white note and likewise takes its name from the white note, such, as B — E , etc.

A natural cancels a sharp or flat.

W. M. Co. 9231

KEY SIGNATURES: When all notes of a certain letter name are to be played sharp or flat, the information is given in the key signature appearing at the beginning of the measure.

MAJOR SCALES

In "Parallel" Scales, the notation is the same, but the Key Signatures are different.

6

MINOR SCALES

KEY SIGNATURES:

Terms of Speed (or pace)—
Largo......*very slow.*
Lento......*very slow.*
Adagio.....*slow.*
Andante....*moderately slow.*
Andantino..*not quite as slow as andante.*
Moderato...*at moderate pace.*
Allegretto...*moderately fast.*
Allegro.....*fast.*
Presto......*very fast.*

Terms of Power or Intensity—
Pianissimo..*(pp) very soft.*
Piano......*(p) soft.*
Mezzo-forte.*(mf), moderately loud.*
Forte......*(f) loud.*
Fortissimo..*(ff), very loud.*
Crescendo...*growing lounder.*
Decrescendo.*growing softer.*
Diminuendo.*growing softer.*
Sforzando...*suddenly loud.*
Subito piano.*suddenly soft.*

Terms of Changing Speed—
Accellerando..*becoming faster.*
Rallentando..*becoming slower.*
Ritardando...*becoming slower.*
Ritenuto....*becoming slower.*
Piu mosso....*more motion, faster.*
Meno mosso..*less motion, slower.*
A tempo......*resume pace, after a retard.*
Rubato.......*not too strict.*

Terms of Style or Character—
Amimato..........*with spirit.*
Assai.............*enough.*
Cantabile..........*song-like.*
Con..............*with.*
Dolce.............*sweetly.*
Espressivo.........*with expression.*
Grazia............*gracefully*
Legato.............*continuous flow of sound from tone to tone.*
Leggiero..........*lightly.*
Ma non troppo......*but not too much.*
Maestoso..........*majestically, stately.*
Marcato...........*well marked.*
Molto.............*much.*
Pesante...........*heavy.*
Poco.............*a little.*
Portamento.........*(on the piano), tones slightly detached, semi-staccato.*
Portamento.........*(on the violin or voice), smooth gliding from tone to tone.*
Scherzando.........*playfully.*
Senza.............*without.*
Sostenuto..........*well sustained.*
Staccato...........*very detached, disconnected tones indicated by dots over or under the notes.*
Subito............*suddenly.*
Vivo (or vivace).....*lively.*
Tranquillo (or vivace).*quietly.*

Terms and Signs used in Notation—

A cappella, without accompaniment.

Accent (> ʌ), extra stress or emphasis.

Al segno (𝄋), repeat *to* this sign.

Arpeggio (𝄐), indicates that the tones of the chord which follows the sign are to be produced in rapid succession instead of simultaneously.

Crescendo (———), growing louder.

Da capo (D.C.), repeat from the beginning.

Dal segno (𝄋), repeat *from* this sign.

Decrescendo (———), growing softer.

Diminuendo (———), growing softer.

Dot (•), over or under a note indicates staccato.

After a note (or rest) it lengthens the preceding note (or rest) by one half the time-value of the note (or rest).

Fermata (⌢), a sign indicating that the tone or rest under it is to be prolonged beyond its prescribed duration. (It is also called a pause or a hold.)

Fine, or finis, the end.

Grace-note (♪), a rapid embellishment of one or more notes preceding the principal note. It is usually printed in small type and played without time-value.

Inverted mordent (𝆭), a rapid embellishment consisting of the principal tone, the scale tone above it and the principal tone again.

Mordent (𝆮), a rapid embellishment consisting of the principal tone, the scale tone below it and the principal tone again.

Opus, a work or composition.

Ottava (*8......*), indicates that the notes under the dotted line are to be played one octave higher than written, or those over the dotted line are to be played one octave lower than written.

Ped. (pedal), indicates the use of the damper pedal until the sign for its release ✻ · Other forms of pedal markings are ⌐_____⌐ and ⌐_____⌐.

Phrasing, bringing out the phrases of a composition by means of proper expression.

Score, the complete notation of all the music played by all the instruments in a composition.

Syncopation, the placing of accented tones between accented beats instead of coinciding with them. It is caused by prolonging the tone on the weak beat through the succeeding accented beat (which is suppressed).

Tie ⌢, a curved line placed over (or under) two successive notes of the same pitch, by which the time-value of the first is made to include that of the second without repetition.

Time, the number and division of rhythmic beats within a measure.

Time signature, the numerical fraction placed on the staff at the beginning of a composition or section of a composition to indicate the number of beats in a measure and the time-value of each beat.

Transpose, to change a composition from the key in which it is written to another key.

Trill (*tr⌁*), a sign indicating the rapid alternation of a principal tone with the tone a half- or a whole-step above it, lasting for the duration of the principal tone.

Triplet, the division of a beat (or part of a beat) into three equal parts of the next smaller time-value.

Turn (∾), a rapid embellishment of four tones, the second and fourth being the principal tone, or written note, and the first and third being the scale tones immediately above and below it.

Tre corde, (three strings), without soft pedal.

Una corda (one string) with soft pedal.

CLASSIFICATION OF VOICES

The three main types in women's voices are usually considered: Soprano, Mezzo-Soprano and Alto. Here is shown the average range of each.

Soprano

Mezzo-Soprano

Alto

The three main types in men's voices are usually considered: Tenor, Baritone and Bass. Here is shown the average range of each.

Tenor

Baritone

Bass
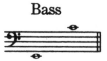